The Church's Mightiest
Weapon Released

Books by Paul J. Bucknell

Allowing the Bible to speak to our lives today!

- *Overcoming Anxiety: Finding Peace, Discovering God*
- *Reaching Beyond Mediocrity: Faith's Triumph Over Temptation*
- *The Life Core: Discovering the Heart of Great Training*
- *Life in the Spirit! Experiencing the Fullness of Christ*
- *The Church's Mightiest Weapon Released: A strategic plan to unite the church...*
- *The Making of A Godly Leader: Isaiah 53, The Fourth Servant Song*
- *An Examination of Our Theological Conclusions*
- *The Godly Man: When God Touches a Man's Life*
- *Redemption Through the Scriptures/ Study Guide*
- *Godly Beginnings for the Family*
- *Principles and Practices of Biblical Parenting*
- *Building a Great Marriage*
- *The Lord Your Healer: Discover Him and Find...*
- *Christian Premarital Counseling Manual for Counselors*
- *Relational Discipleship: Cross Training*
- *A Biblical Perspective of Social Justice Issues*
- *A Spiritual Map for Unity*
- *The Origins of the Bible*
- *Running the Race: Overcoming Lusts*
- *The Bible Teaching Commentary on Genesis*
- *The Bible Teaching Commentary on Romans*
- *Book of Romans: Bible Study Questions*
- *Book of Ephesians: Bible Studies*
- *Walking with Jesus: Abiding in Christ*
- *Inductive Bible Studies in Titus*
- *Life Transformation: A Monthly ... on Romans 12:9-21*
- *1 Peter Bible Study Questions: Living in a Fallen World*
- *Satan's Four Stations: The Destroyer is Destroyed*
- *3 X E Discipleship (Discipler and Disciple)*
- *Take Your Next Step into Ministry*
- *Training Leaders for Ministry*
- *Study Guide for Jonah: Understanding God's Heart*

Check out our Discipleship Digital Libraries at www.foundationsforfreedom.net

The Church's Mightiest Weapon Released

A strategic plan to unite the church
and reach the nations to glorify God

Paul J. Bucknell

Book Information

The Church's Mightiest Weapon Released: A strategic plan to unite the church and reach the nations to glorify God

Copyright © 2023 by Paul J. Bucknell
ISBN: 978-1-61993-195-4 (Paperback)

Digital format:
ISBN: 978-1-61993-196-1
https://bffbible.org
https://www.foundationsforfreedom.net

The NASB version is used unless otherwise stated.
New American Standard Bible ©1960, 1995 used by permission, Lockman Foundation www.lockman.org.

Paul J. Bucknell, USA

Paul authored this book and only used AI's assistance for editing.

Tribute

Praise Jesus, the Apostle and High Priest, the true Builder of God's house, His people!

> For He has been counted worthy of more glory than Moses, by just so much as the builder of the house has more honor than the house. For every house is built by someone, but the builder of all things is God. (Heb 3:3-4)

Nowhere is God's patient and longstanding grace more clearly seen than in His willingness to work with His divisive, prideful, and obstinate people. May His grace like a river pour through the church's arteries, manifesting the great love of God.

Appreciation

Thanks to Joshua del Real for the cover idea and the background artwork.

Table of Contents

An Introduction

The church's greatest weapon is unity, but unfortunately, we have only detected small, thumbnail glimpses of the beauty of this state. The church's glaring disunity hinders the fulfillment of the Great Commission; we are too divided to muster enough strength and determination to strike the enemy. An insidious darkness has been planted within the weak church.

This fast-closing age leaves only a brief period for the church to unleash her most powerful weapon of unity. Only a concentrated effort of Spirit-initiated oneness will crack the unwieldy barriers of disunity in the church, strategically paving the way to reach the world.

Recently, when sharing with a pastor my recent burden for regaining the church's unity, he asked, "What does this unity look like?" I didn't have a satisfactory answer. At that point, I could only share how difficult it is for someone who grew up in a dysfunctional family (me) to share what a good family looks like and how it operates. The Lord graciously used one unity project from another forthcoming book, _An Examination of Our Theological Conclusions_, to provide the needed insights for this book. Despite our present factions, doubt, haughtiness, and disappointments, the church can step up and magnificently display her unity and complete the task Jesus gave her to reach the lost. I welcome you to carefully scrutinize the strategy proposed in this book against God's Word.

This is a critical time for the church. The circumstances accompanying the pandemic devastated the church. While many churches have returned to some state of normalcy, numerous ones have not returned. I believe our precarious world is again seeking to test the church worldwide. Whether you agree that we are seeing signs signaling the final days before Jesus' return, it doesn't matter. The Great Harlot is trampling about us, force-feeding immorality to us (Rev 17:1); the United Nations launched a new world religion centered around the "sin" of carbon footprints to appease climate change activists. World governments are recklessly in debt. CBDCs (i.e., cashless societies) are already being implemented in certain places, giving the elitists further control over people's financial affairs through social credits.

This book is necessarily brief, yet it provides the biblically-based vision and means for today's churches to display her glorious unity, that which is "good and acceptable and perfect" (Rom 12:2). I'm asking you to pray and pass on copies of this book as God guides you (at no cost).[1]

After outlining the concise biblical perspective of church unity and its significance, I present a plan on how the church can boldly display unity and simultaneously safeguard God's flock. The book concludes by enumerating the advantages of this plan and answering many common questions regarding unity in the church. Later in the book, we link to an updated web page on

---

[1] Resources for this book: https://bffbible.org/d1/view/church-unity-resources

upcoming resources to implement this plan. Feel free to contribute to this list of resources.[2]

I am very aware that unless the Spirit of God powerfully awakens and leads His pastors and church, this plan will not work. But "The LORD is exalted, for He dwells on high" (Isaiah 33:5). Jesus Christ, as our king and Chief Shepherd, seeks to display His desire to care for His sheep and save the lost. May we, the church of God, be motivated by God's will rather than the many pressures and pleasures around us.

> And He will be the stability of your times, a wealth of salvation, wisdom and knowledge; the fear of the LORD is his treasure. (Isaiah 33:6)

Paul J. Bucknell

September 2023, USA

---

[2] Email me at info@bffbible.org.

Section 1:
The Vision for the Church's Unity

Visions and strategies for the church must be based on God's Word. When we receive His wisdom and follow His guidance, our renewed minds can work toward achieving the church's unity as distinctly instructed in His Word. It is critical to value Christ's bride's unity and work together around what unites us—Jesus Christ—rather than what divides us.

Three aspects of the church's unity highlight its biblical support and teaching.

The Commands for Church Unity

The New Testament letters repeatedly command God's people to love one another, preserve unity, live in harmony, confess sins of pride and division, and exhort to seek harmony. Among our many disputes as a global church, we don't argue over these commands! I'll briefly introduce four of them.

Love one another: "A new commandment I (Jesus) give to you, that you love one another, even as I have loved you, that you also love one another" (John 13:34). Christ's presence in our lives activates a greater and more fervent love.[3] When we love others in the way Christ commands, God helps us better understand the Christ's deep,

---

[3] The word "love" is used 234 times in the New Testament.

incredible love (Eph 3:18-19), which spurs us to accomplish God's goals for us and the world.

Preserve unity: "Being diligent **to preserve** the unity of the Spirit in the bond of peace" (Eph 4:3). The Spirit has already knitted the body of Christ together as one. Unity is the backbone of the church's spiritual nature, drawing our hearts to fellowship with other believers (Eph 4:1; 2 Cor 12:20). Division is evidence of our missing faith, but this lack of faith does not disprove the truth of the Lord's vision for the church's unity. This is similar to Jesus' comment on marriage: "What therefore God has joined together, let no man separate" (Matt 19:6). Let's give no ground to disunity but instead seek to display unity.

Confess sin: According to Ephesians 4:31, it's essential to eliminate **all** bitterness, wrath, anger, clamor, slander, and malice. These sinful attitudes and behaviors damage our relationships and deceive us into believing that our opinions and beliefs are superior to the beliefs and opinions of others. When we let these attitudes reign, we start to believe that we do not need community—but this distorts the truth. By letting go of our sinful ways through Christ's mercy, we can work together to honor our Lord and follow His guidance. We must value every believer as an essential and strategic body member.

Restore harmony: "With all humility and gentleness, with patience, showing tolerance for one another in love" (Eph 4:2). "Be kind to one another, tender-hearted, forgiving each other, just as God in Christ also has forgiven you" (Eph 4:32). These commands directly challenge us to live in light of the love God has shown us.

In summary, Christ made us one body and thus urges us to live according to that truth, disregarding all other views. Those who seek the success of our Lord's plans will experience the powerful benefits of unity and joyful collaboration.

The Example of Church Unity

The apostles and early church leaders gathered together to mark the Feast of Pentecost following His resurrection: "all with one mind," "continually devoting themselves to prayer" (Acts 1:14). The seismic change in the church happened when Christ's Spirit infilled the church as she met in one accord. The Holy Spirit filled his people and used them to release a powerful and timely burst of evangelistic preaching. They gathered in believers' homes, discipling many new believers. The Pentecost harvest following the spring rains symbolizes the actual spiritual harvest. The many new foreign-born believers soon returned to their homelands, testifying of Jesus' love and sharing God's mighty acts to the far reaches of the world.

Just as the church gathered together by the Lord's instruction to usher in the "first rains" (Acts 1:17-21) prophesied by Joel (Joel 2:28-32),[4] God now seeks to gather His church to welcome the "second rains" before the very last set of Jewish Feasts in the redemptive calendar, the Feast of the Tabernacles.[5] We anticipate God

---

[4] Joel 2:23 mentions the early and latter rains in reference to the rainy seasons before the early and late harvests, which tells us that this is God's plan before the final harvest, seeing how He did it with Pentecost.

[5] To be consistent, perhaps, like in the first prophetic sequence, there will be a great atonement (feast #6) preceding this final Feast of Booths. Will this include our grief for our blindness to our disunity?

again will pour out His Spirit for this latter harvest, encouraging His people across the globe to gather "all with one mind."[6]

The truth of this illustration lies not in my interpretation of the Old Testament redemptive calendar (which you can disagree with) but in Jesus' words, "This gospel of the kingdom shall be preached in the whole world as a testimony to all the nations, and then the end will come" (Matt 24:14; Daniel 12:1-4). Jesus' Great Commission heralds us to boldly live and proclaim His Gospel to the ends of the world (Matt 28:18-20).

God seeks to restore our unity, further anoint His people, and enable us to complete His global mission. As His people, start praying for your neighbors no matter where you live. Find God's people and pray together for unity as often as possible. One unique feature of revival movements is how the number of believers multiplied. Still, another unique feature is the unity that the body of Christ experienced during that time, seen in cross-denomination fellowship and worship. Does the revival come first and then these signs or do the people God need to have oneness of mind to invite revival? I think the latter.

---

[6] This is not a subtle reference to a new revival of tongues; God will spread the Gospel in His sovereign way.

The Meaning of Church Unity

God saves us through faith in Christ and makes us one body where we must mutually work together to complete God's good purposes. Unity describes the nature of the church and the joint participation of her members to follow Jesus' instructions. God's children are born again into a united family, empowered by the Holy Spirit to glorify the Father by carrying out His will.

God's church looks vastly different now compared to the times of the early church. Now filled with many large and small denominational enclaves, the organization of its parts has overwhelmed the organism, despoiling the church's innate beauty. Believers everywhere tolerate division over doctrine, liturgy, leaders, etc., even the Lord's supper!

Disunity is a spiritual stronghold on the church.

Despite our errors over the centuries, the Lord has graciously aided the church in her mission to spread His saving Gospel to many people groups worldwide (Matt 28:18-19). However, we cannot complete this mission without joining together in heart and vision. It takes all of us.

The church's steps toward unity, such as planning, training, and meeting together in one accord, welcome the Spirit of God to powerfully work in and through her—and not just at one central place but across the globe. What a testimony! May God's kingdom come on earth even as it is in heaven.

In the following section, I will provide a strategic plan for how the church can display her unity. I'm not advocating for large group meetings but for small, local home meetings styled after those of the early church with an important tweak.

Section 2:
The Plan for the Church's Unity

It's easy to recite the Apostles' Creed, "I believe in… the holy catholic church, the communion of saints…,"[7] but how should the church act as one and display her unity in light of all the differences among her members? Although the Lord again released the Word of God and teachings of salvation during the Reformation, faith in her unity was stolen, undermining her power.[8]

Unity and love are the most powerful weapons in the church's arsenal, standing in stark contrast to the world's acute divisiveness. "By this all men will know that you are My disciples, if you have love for one another" (John 13:35). While we can individually pray or memorize God's Word, the devil trembles when we congregate in harmony to pray and worship (Neh 8:1-12). We have seen hints of unity during times of revival and worship, but the Lord calls us to deliberately unite in joint adoration and service.

Mostly, we have congregated around our differences rather than the reason for our unity. We worship with those of the same doctrine, liturgy, worship style, etc., but God is doing something much larger and wants us, His people, to meet around and for Jesus Christ. I know we have justified our

---

[7] From the Apostles' Creed. "Catholic" means universal, all-inclusive.

[8] Of course, though the evil one sowed the temptations, God's people in the end made the decisions to break from other believers over doctrines. We confused purity with doctrinal isolationism.

factions with convincing arguments, and yet, the results are the same—we remain separated from each other, conducting church in our own comfortable bubbles, away from those who do church differently than us, rather than repenting from our divisiveness.

Church organizations have clouded the church's true identity, mission, and allegiance to Christ. Our formalized structures have separated our hearts and minds from our brethren, especially those with different secondary doctrines.

We have been unable to untie this tight knot of disharmony and mistrust, which I suspect is because we have neither resolved long-held bitterness (Heb 12:15) nor addressed the problems associated with prolonged pride and wealth.

We Still Have a Choice

How can we demonstrate and live out our unity? We must meet and operate together under our one Lord! It's an important concept made more powerful by action, as the early church showed us. Since the Reformation, Christians have largely promoted meetings within their selective groups, but this direction doesn't display genuine unity. Though sincere, they are still factions. It is true that God's people often become mobilized to support certain issues (e.g., preserving the lives of the unborn), to worship at a concert, or to teach or go on mission (e.g., Urbana), but these attempts are far too limited in scope, rarely last more than a few days, and can be cost prohibitive, excluding many.

I'm calling Christians everywhere to meet where they live, not according to their denominations and church groups. Most important to note is that if we are proactive, we don't need to disrupt or threaten existing churches but bless them. We can meet at a different time, like Sunday or a weekday evening, for a short designated time, like three weeks.

The church was utterly unprepared for the last pandemic, which resulted in many believers not meeting. The sheep were scattered. Why not prepare now for such times? We must care for the sheep, especially considering the weak, weary, and wounded. We might face similar trials to the seven churches in Revelation. Some countries in Africa, for example, did not face any restrictions or dangers during the recent worldwide pandemic. However, past events serve as warning signs that point to further world-scale dangers.

Some places, like China, have already experienced the power of home fellowships. Despite harsh persecution, the Chinese church grew mightily. Whether temporarily or for a long time, we may see more occasions for similar lockdowns or emergencies that render the church unable to meet as usual. Our Lord can use these societal upsets, including war and famine, to herd us toward genuine unity. This plan guides us to obey our Great Shepherd's words of love and unity.

God has designed us to display His glory through our unity. Instead of being isolated during times of crisis, scattered, bruised, and disillusioned by what we see on our screens, the church can continue to meet under preappointed, qualified, and equipped leaders in every locale worldwide! They would not meet according to doctrinal and liturgical differences, but in small neighborhood groups formed around Jesus Christ and His powerful saving work on the cross and His resurrection. This is just what happened at Pentecost—Jesus is alive!

Proactive Planning

Proactive planning prepares God's people by briefly setting up and meeting in local neighborhood groups. The plan establishes the church's unity in two ways: it (1) trains and appoints qualified leaders and (2) oversees the distribution and care for each group of God's sheep.

Display the Unity of the Church

 At the Church Leadership Level — Coordinate home groups across church borders according to where they live.

 At the Believers' Worship Level — Worship in home groups with local neighbors.

Unity Is Importantly displayed at two levels.

The general plan is for all Christian church pastors/key elders in a region (e.g., parts of a city) to choose leaders from their churches, equip them, and assign them to lead groups based on where they live. The same regional leaders will group members from local churches according to their neighborhoods and set them up with a nearby leader.

The church leaders in each region will meet under the call of God and unite for joint prayer, planning, and training in anticipation of greater opportunities to reach their region for Christ. These leaders will meet to put this plan into motion on two levels: training leaders and overseeing the gathering of members with their assigned home groups in their neighborhoods. (Also, see Appendix 1.)

For example, a local church's trained and qualified leaders might each lead a home group that is made up of members from different churches who live in the same area as the group leader. The neighborhood is that group's meeting place and mission field. Like each of Israel's tribes, the group assumes responsibility for their neighborhood area.

Vision leads, not convenience or tradition. Churches must plan for dire, urgent societal situations, and with the leadership of our risen Lord, these plans can be used in mighty ways. As a result of being part of this kind of group, God's people may enjoy the opportunity to know their fellow neighbors and worship together across dividing lines. Moreover, the presence of these groups can proclaim the unity of Christ's body in their neighborhoods. Each community group has the opportunity to shine God's light and love in their neighborhood. As God's people meet in oneness across the land, they can rejoice in the wisdom and care of their leaders.

Training Leaders

Regional church leaders must first choose, instill a vision, equip, and train home group leaders from their churches.

Each regional district will look different, depending on how many believers are in the area, how spread apart they are, and whether they are in a city or rural setting. These leaders must intentionally worship and serve the King and Great Shepherd; He is in charge.

Though these home groups are meant to be temporary, they might, if due to emergency or helpfulness, continue. If this happens, it is vital to ensure qualified overseers are in place, as these home groups would function as a church in such cases. Some churches admittedly have a head start here, thanks to active home group leaders and experienced pastors. Strong and equipped leaders must assist pastors and churches that don't have well-trained leaders. This will increase the number of qualified and trained leaders and will strengthen the whole church.[9] We often expect larger churches to naturally have more leaders, but size is not the best indicator. More important is whether they hold leadership training.

Being proactive allows the district pastor/home leaders to better know their fellow pastors and leaders and build mutual trust. All leaders must openly affirm their loyalty to the Gospel of Christ (their personal faith) and commit to studying God's Word (methodology). Acceptance of the Apostles Creed or an agreed-upon basic Gospel confession (1 Cor 15:1-4) assures these leaders' loyalty to the Gospel as presented in the Bible. Each home group will have one designated leader and possible assistants as appropriate. Some leaders may need to oversee multiple

---

[9] As an international church planter and former pastor of a church for college students and professors, training leaders has been the backbone of my ministry because their time at our church was typically only a few years.

groups before assigning a regular leader. Those who show leadership potential should be noted and receive ongoing developmental training.

By meeting, worshiping, and praying with other leaders, mutual trust is built as they acquire God's vision for their neighborhoods. Whatever their positions at their local churches, they are volunteers when leading the three suggested home meetings. Titles, if necessary, can be "Brother" or "Pastor," depending largely on cultural expectations and training. The attendees should continue their commitments to their existing churches as much as possible. Churches with weekly small group meetings or other programs should temporarily adjust their schedules to accommodate these neighborhood group sessions and all the training needed to run them.

The regional church leaders need to devise a group organization plan. They are responsible for determining where all the leaders and believers live and divvying them up among groups on one map according to where they live. Believers will not group according to their church affiliation but their neighborhood location, near a group leader. The neighborhood could be small or large but preferably within a mile circumference, with an average of fifteen adults per group. If believers are in a dense city, holding multiple group meetings in the same building is possible to keep the group sizes manageable.

The distribution of believers into groups will require special prayer and planning. One advantage of such deep-level strategic planning is the ability to identify areas with very few or no believers. This is one problem that the broader team of leaders should try to solve proactively. One or more existing local churches can send evangelistic teams to that unreached district, or a few believers with a burdened leader can move into that area, if only temporarily.

It's easy for the evil one to stir up envy, mistrust, and even pride in our time. Having a strategic plan can subdue many fears and insecurities because it keeps believers focused on God's greater goal.

Being proactive means church leaders will display their unity by prayerfully working together under Christ's leadership and the Holy Spirit's guidance. Though each regional area will need one or more volunteer administrative coordinators to distribute and send notices, this is not a position of authority and would likely be temporary.[10] Established pastor leaders must learn to make decisions together under Jesus Christ's rule, keeping His goals in mind. The appointment of trained leaders helps assure pastors that their sheep can be cared for in distressful times. Unity is exemplified when these trained leaders work together with other churches and Christians.

> "We, the pastors of _____ are one in Christ and appoint these leaders to care for this regional church through neighborhood Christian groups."

The church leaders' proactive training and planning will serve as the first mighty demonstration of unity, affirming that the local church consists of one group of pastors and

---

[10] Lists can be dangerous if there is hostility toward believers, especially in this digital world. However, maintaining lists can be advantageous because they make it easier to watch whether groups struggle or grow. The regional leaders must together evaluate the situation and conclude the best approach.

leaders working together under the Chief Shepherd to care for God's flock.

> Behold, how good and how pleasant it is
> For brothers to dwell together in unity! (Psalm 133:1)

What a powerful statement from the psalmist! This joint effort is a beacon of light from the Lord to churches, unbelievers, and the dark world alike. As the Light shines, fellowships grow. God will powerfully use this effort to anoint His people and enable the church to seek the lost and cripple the evil one's plans.

The church wields her most powerful weapon—unity— when leaders pray and plan with one mind under the Lord Jesus Christ to care for the needs of the sheep.

Gathering Together

By their very nature, the home groups powerfully bear witness to the church's unity because they, as God's people, meet irrespective of denomination and other differences. The home groups should plan to meet only three times initially—for example, on the first Sunday evening of the month for three months, or three consecutive Wednesdays. These meetings, which do not detract from the established local churches, enable leaders and worshippers alike to work through the kinks and discover the benefits of meeting neighborhood Christians and seekers. Those attending the home group will resolve most local issues that arise.

Local leaders can meet with other nearby leaders for mutual support and mentorship as needed (Titus 2:2).

Leaders and believers will bathe their meetings in prayer. Pastors of existing churches should follow up with their appointed home group leaders and see how each group went, helping as needed.

The overall coordinators can kick off the distribution plan by contacting the set home group leaders and their overseeing church pastor during the initial setup. He will provide the attendees' contact information to the group leaders, and the location of group members will be plotted on a map. Members will be notified in two ways.

First, their existing pastor will share an overview of this plan with their members, encourage them with additional information, and introduce them to their leader. Second, the home group leader will personally invite each assigned member to their neighborhood's first home fellowship meeting.

We will see great results with little effort. People living close by can mutually help and befriend each other—even without continued official meetings. It's an instant community. The presence of this community should be an opportunity for the many stray sheep, perhaps those who stopped attending due to the pandemic, to return to the Lord as the group begins to pray for and reach their neighborhoods. The local home group should prayerfully visit other neighbors to see if other neighbors are interested in attending. As God leads, they can plan and finance local activities like a barbecue block party, etc. Each community group will know what best works among those living in their area and will care for their own expenses.

Once the vision for their neighborhood is established, the trusted local community will continue to work together, especially in times of great need. It will be much easier to plan, pray, and reach out when the people know each other, even if it's once a year—though we hope unofficial neighborhood prayer meetings continue.

The initial fellowship meetings are planned to occur for three weeks. Leaders and members can invite new responsive contacts to their existing churches. If an emergency occurs in the future, these home groups will be ready to meet and support each other. They already know each other! The hope is that the group will expand as each welcomes, prays for, and cares for believing and unbelieving neighbors.

If we are proactive, we can quickly alleviate many problems facing these plans, which gives us more time to pray through issues and build mutual trust among leaders and members. Further instruction and training can be given once gifted, qualified, and willing home group leaders are identified.

Leaders need not preach a 45-minute message! Proper training and Bible studies can be organized beforehand, decreasing the concern over what topics might be selected for discussion. For example, the first meetings' studies might be on Psalm 23 or on the Lord's Prayer as a guiding discussion text. After reading the Bible passage, the leader can spend ten or fifteen minutes to share his thoughts, and then others can share spontaneous responses (1 Cor 14:26). Provided study questions can be used as time allows. Make sure to allot time for joint worship and prayer for the members' concerns and the neighborhood, perhaps on a theme relevant to the study text. During these times, let us come together as a united community, across different churches, to express gratitude to God for Jesus Christ, our Savior and Lord.

The biggest challenge will be for leaders to trust other leaders. To encourage this trust, you can use special exercises designed to build trust. The attendees will likely be less concerned with meeting with other believers, especially if their pastor recommends it. Despite the obstacles these home groups might encounter, their meetings can powerfully demonstrate the church's unity, allowing the love and light of Jesus to spread to their neighbors.

Our hope is for these home groups to become mission-minded because they realize their need to pray for, love, and witness to their unbelieving neighbors. Some neighbors might not be interested, but people will likely grow in interest during tumultuous times. Moreover, people are always looking for love; someone going through a tough time might reach out to someone in the group, asking them to pray for their concerns. These groups are meant to be powerful lighthouses for God, and though they officially will only meet a few times, the friendships and bonds can last forever.

Preemptive Planning

Preemptive planning happens when proactive planning has not been prioritized. Pastors might quickly realize how important it is for their members to have these small neighborhood groups after difficult circumstances have arisen. The distressing circumstances might help them see their members meeting with other professing believers is much better than being alone or preyed on by wolves.

Preemptive planning is an oxymoron, as it is more of a direct response to a current threat than a strategy prepared before it was needed. Organizations tend to be inept in providing good care because they do not prepare for the worst, which allows the enemy to trouble them further. Organizational pride, rules, and culture may inhibit the planning and implementation of these neighborhood groups. During the pandemic, most believers did not meet with others, even in their local areas. Consider what your pastors did during the pandemic. What happened to the flock they were charged with? I hope we can kindly critique one's situation to better prepare ourselves for the next challenging event. God's people are sheep and need someone to lead them in dangerous times.

It may not be possible to solve the looming large-scale problems with the same strategies the church used before. What if YouTube and Facebook censor online Christian meetings, the internet is hacked, or the electricity grid goes down? What worked for the COVID-19 pandemic may not be a good backup plan next time around. If pastors take action to set up these groups now, the people will know what to do when the time comes. They will be instantly prepared to meet with other neighborhood Christians in prayer and fellowship. Pastors should encourage their members to meet regularly with their neighborhood groups, yet, without trusted leaders, it can be understandably hard for pastors to bless the meetings.

The pandemic stands as a reminder of the scale of difficulties we may face as believers. Without planning, training, and strategy, the situation can quickly become messy, allowing for unnecessary confusion and pain. To get a feel for what it's like to help fledgling churches read through the Book of Titus so you can get a feel for dealing with problems caused by a lack of supervision.[11]

Summary

When positioned correctly, the church can proactively achieve unity on two levels: leaders declare unity at the leadership level by working together and believers demonstrate it in home group meetings. By God's grace, the church will enthusiastically engage in this process and shine forth God's love and truth.

---

[11] Book of Titus: https://www.foundationsforfreedom.net/References/NT/Pauline/Titus/Titus1/Titus1_1a_Paul-Titles.html

Section 3:
The Advantages of Church Unity

There are numerous advantages to locally meeting in neighborhood *koinonia* groups to worship God, celebrate Christ, study God's Word, and love our neighbors for Christ, even if only for a brief three-week period.

The Advantages of Selecting Group Leaders

- Existing churches will have qualified and trusted leaders, trained in how the Scriptures teach (Titus 1:5-8).

- Good training programs adequately prepare leaders and provide, under the eyes of present leaders, to spot and train up new leaders.

- Home group leaders can meet together under the mentorship of a more experienced leader/pastor.

- Existing churches gain more experienced leaders and people who better understand how to reach out to their neighbors.

- Leaders across local churches can fellowship together and consider how they may more effectively shine God's light in their communities.

- Unreached areas are easily detected and targeted.

- Leaders can strategically pray for the region and its needs rather than generally praying for the welfare of the existing local church.

- Leader meetings are excellent opportunities for the Holy Spirit to break down barriers like pride and bitterness and provide opportunities for reconciliation across the board.

- Home group leaders can foster friendships with other nearby leaders.

- Pastors and church leaders can, in faith, know they are protecting their appointed sheep no matter what persecution or calamities strike.

- Leaders are better equipped to rely on God and confidently lead God's people, even when society becomes hostile to established churches (debanking or censoring them).

- Pastors can be involved by (1) checking in with congregants to hear how their home groups went, and (2) working closely with the home group leaders under their authority.

The Advantages of Neighborhood Groups

- God's Spirit can refresh the faith of His people as they meet and worship with other nearby believers.

- Neighborhood home groups have organic opportunities to share the Gospel and show the love of Jesus to neighbors.

- Christians can show their love to their neighbors in a personal way rather than relying on impersonal organizations, such as food shelters. (They could also work together with organizations!)

- Believers can explore and better utilize their spiritual gifts daily, learning to value each member of the body of Christ.

- The ministry of God's Word and worship in these times can nurture believers beyond their usual participation in church activities.

- Christians can expand their vision on how to better minister as God's priests in prayer and service (1 Peter 2:5,9).

- Believers can get to know neighbors better and establish a trusted community and support base, which is critical during uncertain times and always rewarding, made up of believers and unbelievers alike.

- Home groups can function well in both bountiful times and in times of persecution because of their members' mutual support and concern.

- Home groups are God-centered, providing personal interactions and genuine friendships (1 John 1:3-4).

- These groups can communicate easily, without modern digital devices and vehicles, if necessary.

- These groups are flexible and can grow and divide easily with proven new and upcoming leaders.

- These groups can easily adjust times and meeting places to facilitate their group's needs and security.

- They are self-sufficient, needing no government registration or outside financing.

Imagine a neighborhood with seventy-five houses, one trained leader, and fifteen believers. The trained leader finds two assistants. The plan I've outlined in the pages above sets up an opportunity for these believers to meet for only three weeks, but the believers in this neighborhood can continue to meet and start strategically praying and planning with other local believers as God leads them. The evil one's plans will be frustrated as many of the disenchanted believers and unbelievers in the neighborhood witness the love of God among His people, restoring hope in Christ through the church lived out in community.

> 9 But you are a chosen race, a royal priesthood, a holy nation, a people for God's own possession, so that you may proclaim the excellencies of Him who has called you out of darkness into His marvelous light; 10 for you once were not a people, but now you are the people of God; you had not received mercy, but now you have received mercy. (1 Peter 2:9-10)

Section 4:
Questions and Answers

The presentation of this plan will raise many questions. I've been involved in several church plants and have worked with churches around the globe, so I think it's safe to say that I'm familiar with much of the pushback this type of plan can receive. I can explain more, but the best way to stay updated on further developments for the plan is to follow this web page for more resources, including a free copy of this book to download, videos, training schemes, Bible studies, implementation suggestions, testimonies, etc.[12] I'm hoping others can freely contribute their suggestions, translations, etc. as they work through the process. I've intentionally kept this book brief to hasten the passing of the vision.

- **Why do you think unity is the key to reaching the world for Christ?**

Jesus, Paul, Peter, and John all portray how evil and light intensify at the age's end. The church's unwillingness to live in unity reveals a solidified spiritual stronghold restraining God's people. When strongholds come down, God's love and light powerfully shine in, bringing renewal and revival. Displays of unity, like in Acts 1-2, are how God

---

[12] Resources: https://bffbible.org/d1/view/church-unity-resources

spiritually renews and invigorates us to complete His work. This calls for the church not to work harder but follow the Spirit's leading. Revival and unity are symbiotic and must grow together.

- **Why do you think the movement toward unity is something God is doing now?**

God has recently placed it on my heart and mind. I've been praying (as have many others) for a global revival for a long time, but only now has He helped me understand a plan for how the church can come into this renewal. This plan also appears to be a timely part of a larger puzzle the Lord is assembling to prepare His people for increased times of repression and persecution. As His people catch this vision for unity, they will get excited to see God work and thus will be more willing to work together. Jesus' command for unity has been with us from the beginning. The plan helps the formal church transition into an excited nurturing and missional state.

- **The Lord has charged pastors to guard the flock, so isn't it irresponsible to turn the flock over to others outside of direct church leadership?**

This question is valid. The Lord charged His under-shepherds to feed His sheep. "Shepherd My sheep" (John 21:16). Peter passed this charge on to other shepherds:

> Shepherd the flock of God among you, exercising oversight not under compulsion, but voluntarily, according to the will of God; and not for sordid gain, but with eagerness. (1 Peter 5:2)

Distressful times, however, are looming, especially in certain locations. The books of 1 Peter and Hebrews address the scattered disciples (1 Peter 1:1), and we see how God uses difficult times to spread His Word (Acts 8:1,4). This proactive plan is a managed means for existing churches to better care for their sheep and reach out to nearby lost sheep. Pastors train other qualified and gifted leaders to keep God's people close to God and His Word (Eph 4:12). Existing pastors, meanwhile, should also shepherd one or two home groups.

I'm advocating for a set of three meetings. Even though this training is brief, it adequately prepares for hard times —unlike when the pandemic broke worldwide. Proactive care helps overseers consider challenging long-term scenarios, so that immediate care can be provided. Furthermore, this plan is strategic because it grants a vision of unity to your leaders and the flock. Consider the beauty of the unity displayed when believers meet together in local communities! Also, consider how this simple act of assembling gives them the means to seek the straying and lost sheep.

- **Why do you place such emphasis on finishing the Great Commission? Aren't we almost done anyway?**

Do you want the eternal record to show that you almost finished or that you finished the critical task that Jesus gave? Why trivialize people's eternal lives or Jesus' words? Unity is key to making the final conquests because it breaks down unseen spiritual strongholds.

- **Why this plan?**

Pastors are accountable to the Lord, not this plan. May all of God's people seek and follow the Lord where He leads. This is the solution God has laid on my heart, so I invite you to seriously consider the biblical support for this particular strategy and pray for unity.

Obedience. The church says it believes in unity, but it does not display unity. How do you show your cooperation with other believers? In this plan, I propose a way for believers to display the church's unity, which effectively tears down spiritual strongholds.

Welfare. Antagonistic individuals and groups worldwide are openly threatening the church. The pandemic gave us some insight into how societal upheavals and oppression might impact the church. Genuine love and foresight granted by the pandemic should drive her leaders to train and prepare God's people, building up their local networks beyond their existing churches.

Co-existence. The plan does not threaten existing churches but creates a powerful backup plan. I hope the vision of working with the Lord in the truth of the church's unity will overcome our many fears and encourage God's people everywhere to catch a glimpse of His kingdom work.

- **I've caught the vision for unity but am only one believer in a big church. What can I do?**

We are building unity, brick by brick! Support and pray for your leaders. If the Lord has pricked your heart and moved you toward unity, begin to pray on it and seek out believers in your area. Take more walks and speak to your neighbors. In this way, you'll have started to build an informal support network with other believers in your area.

- **Do you think this is the end before Jesus comes?**

It doesn't matter. God's command to live in unity and train our leaders stands, regardless of the circumstances and increased hardships happening before our eyes. Why not ready ourselves for what we see coming down the line? Governments, banks, and companies are starting to censor/freeze the bank accounts and social media accounts of those they don't like. AI, CBCDs, and debanking are recent terms that further warn us of the future. If this is not the end, a purging time is due.

- **What would you say to pastors and theologians who firmly believe they best protect their churches by keeping their people from doctrines and liturgies they teach?**

Unity means we fully accept each brother or sister who confesses Jesus Christ. If God accepts them, then we must too. This plan requires every leader to confess Jesus Christ and love God's Word. This does not mean an acceptance of those who embrace immoral behavior.[13]

I discuss the more complicated issues of doctrinal division in another book, *"An Examination of Our Theological Conclusions"*[14] which explains the tough issues

---

[13] Check out this word study on "sound doctrine." https://bffbible.org/new-testament/view/sound-doctrine-a-word-study-on-sound-teaching

[14] An Examination of Our Theological Conclusions: https://bffbible.org/store/view/examination-theological-conclusions

surrounding traditions, doctrines, and opinions. In summary, we do not achieve purity by separating ourselves from those with other doctrinal convictions but by drawing closer to Christ. The Divider tries to pit those who follow Christ against each other. Jesus Christ, our only Savior, unites us and demands our loyalty.

- **Who are you?**

I'm a teacher of God's Word. I have worked with numerous denominations, but my chief work has been with the Chinese church, overseas and in the USA, for more than forty years as church planter, pastor, and trainer. After starting BFF in 2000, the Lord called me to train pastors in many countries in 2005. I cannot foresee the future, but as a strategist, I largely frame my observations from God's Word.

- **How are you personally planning to handle all the coming distress?**

We need to be realists. With eight children, eight grandchildren (at the moment), and many informal beloved coworkers stretching around the world, this question hits close to home. God called me into this faith ministry back in 2000 and has faithfully provided for me, my family, and the ministry. One of my earlier books and courses is *Overcoming Anxiety, Finding the Peace of God*, in which you can find many of my thoughts on the topic.[15] In short, I must fully trust God even for our tender (and rough) grandchildren. God created us for this generation, so let us

---

[15] I offer a free online course, *Overcoming Anxiety Finding Peace, Discovering God*, that comes with about thirty 15-minute videos or the option to order the book. Please send me your email at info@bffbible.org to sign up if interested.

be fearless. God can care for them better than I can, but we must remain alert in prayer, crying out to Him for help. Faith leads forward, but fears entertain trouble. Someone wisely observed that God provides no armor for our backs.

- How will the pastors support themselves?

This question of financial support is one many pastors and evangelists worldwide face right now. Some will be new to this situation, but God faithfully provides for those He leads. As long as existing churches continue, members should continue to support them. Local believers can give faithful leaders personal gifts as the Scriptures suggest, if the home groups are ongoing. Give personal gifts, as the Lord leads, avoids pressures, government oversight, and taxes. Persecution and other changes in our societies (like fifteen-minute cities) might diminish the need for large buildings and congregational members living far from others. Pastors need to change with the times and trust God to provide for them apart from a salary.

- Do you think a unified church will make it easier for the Antichrist to take over?

The opposite is true. Proactive training and close supervision of the flock give the best protection from the coming deception. The Antichrist plans to use the False Prophet (the second beast) and possible influence from other world religions to deceive the world. Neighborhood house churches with biblically sound leaders, under the accountability of local mentoring, diminish this risk. They can support each other throughout the week. Wolves prey on stray sheep.

- **How does Jesus lead our churches? Isn't He in heaven?**

God's people have much to learn about trusting our resurrected Lord Jesus, who even today leads His people. Jesus the Great Shepherd is ready to teach us when we lean on Him. We won't know all the answers until we together seek the Lord and affirm our loyalty to Him. We must not stand alone but follow Him in Christ's Spirit.

- **Do these house churches threaten the role of denominational churches?**

This plan seeks not to compete with existing local churches and organizations. As long as established churches continue to function, I see much benefit for them by coordinating these leaders and groups. For instance, established churches could easily add new people to their congregations by following up with those involved in the neighborhood outreach. But these efforts must be in harmony with all. God can and has used denominations, but they can easily interfere with God's best plans.

The appointed leaders of the home groups should be part of an existing church and use this small group outreach to nurture believers and reach unbelievers—something many churches have been unable to do. The existing local churches can, as God leads, encourage their house leaders to reach out thoroughly to their neighbors. God's people will flourish as they together seek the glory of the Lord Jesus through unity.

- **Isn't the church too hardened and divided to step into unity?**

I, too, find myself becoming hopeless—until I remember how light disperses darkness. Even small lights of unity will instantly vanquish signs of division and disunity. God-stirred revivals prove the God-given unity of His people. Unfortunately, some must learn from the loss of their wealth and safety. These circumstances will hasten the process of local meetings.

- **Are you speaking of the universal or local churches?**

The Bible speaks of the universal church, all of God's people, chosen and saved through time, as well as the people of God gathered into local gatherings for feeding, protection, and retooling. Jesus is our Chief Shepherd and shepherds all of us into His one flock to be with Him forever. Each believer is part of the body of Christ, but unity manifests from how we relate to other Christians near us. We are engaged in loving God's people and reaching out to a lost world.

- **What if we end up with people in our groups who don't quite fit?**

I'm unsure why this is a specific concern, but let's focus on two possible scenarios I hope to comprehensively address in future articles. The first is cultural differences. In this case, we are to bridge the gaps the best we can, welcoming these believers as valued and important contributors to the group. Sometimes there is enough of a language group to form a local fellowship. That's fine. But if not, an increase in deliberate personal contact helps tremendously in building friendships.[16] The other scenario might go something like this: Sometimes, due to tradition, immoral behavior, or unclear confession, it does not appear that a person knows the Lord. If they attend, consider them a seeker—someone God is spurring to attend. Ask them about their history and interests. Pray for their salvation.

Summary

This plan provides a biblically sound strategy that the church can use to embody her glorious unity and break down the longstanding spiritual strongholds that have greatly hindered the church. A proactive plan provides the best care possible. As dangers and troubles escalate, each group can quickly meet with each other and provide any needed support. Even more, they can reach out to others who suddenly have needs. Each home group will then be able to explore further how to follow their Lord in learning, loving, and worshiping together.

Send other questions to me, Paul, at info@bffbible.org.

16

Afterword

We don't know where our journeys might end. We start with good intentions and move forward in trust. I started writing this book to outline a means to gain the church's unity, but I've realized that the same strategy is a way for the Lord to better care for his flock and reach the lost. I cannot predict how God might use this plan, but it does give us a way to demonstrate our unity. Formidable obstacles remain; spiritual bondage blinds us to this reality. Desperate times are around the corner, so may we take hold of this opportunity to proactively care for God's people. One day, we will reach the place where we will see the universal church worshiping the Lamb together (Revelation 5).

God seeks to work more deeply in our churches and the world. May we welcome God's unique work "in the church and in Christ Jesus." Jesus repeatedly instructed John to care for his flock. We don't know how God will use our small efforts, but at least our generation can boldly declare that we believe in the church's unity and live it out in our neighborhoods.

> [20] Now to Him who is able to do far more abundantly beyond all that we ask or think, according to the power that works within us, [21] to Him be the glory in the church and in Christ Jesus to all generations forever and ever. Amen." (Eph 3:20-21)

Appendix 1

This graphic illustrates the process leaders and believers might be distributed.

Each church sends their qualified leaders to train and serve as home group leaders.

All the churches supply the church members/seekers in one large listing to be distributed in neighborhood small groups.

One leader and maybe assistants are appointed for each area, targeting 15 adult members per small group.

Their location becomes the small group's target area.

About the Author

Paul J. Bucknell

Paul worked as an overseas church planter in Taiwan during the 1980s and pastored in the United States during the 1990s. God called him to establish Biblical Foundations for Freedom (BFF) in 2000. Since then, he has been actively writing, holding international Christian leadership training seminars, and serving in the local church.

Paul's wide range of biblically based books and media-rich training materials on Christian life, discipleship, godly living, unity, leadership training, marriage, parenting, anxiety, Old and New Testament studies, and other spiritual life topics provide many practical insights.

Paul has been married for more than forty-five beautiful years. With eight children and eight grandchildren, Paul and his wife Linda watch God's blessings unfold.

➡ Check online for more information on Paul and Linda and the BFF ministry.[17]

---

[17] https://www.foundationsforfreedom.net/Help/AboutBFF/Biography.html

➡ Or check out his two websites under BFF, Biblical Foundations for Freedom.

www.bffbible.org

www.foundationsforfreedom.net

Made in the USA
Columbia, SC
07 October 2024